Learn Ab

SNOW

by Christopher Hernandez
illustrated by Richard Watson

SCHOLASTIC INC.
NEW YORK TORONTO LONDON AUCKLAND
SYDNEY MEXICO CITY NEW DELHI HONG KONG

FOR MY FAMILY—AS LONG AS YOU LOVE ME SO, LET IT SNOW.

—C.H.

ISBN 978-0-545-41715-0

16 15 14 13 12 17 18

Printed in the U.S.A. 40

First edition, January 2012
Book design by Jennifer Rinaldi Windau

Snow is for . . .

falling on a cold winter day.

Snow is for . . .

riding on your favorite sleigh.

Snow is for . . .

rolling into a ball just like this.

Snow is for . . .

throwing—make sure not to miss!

Snow is for . . .

making a new friend just like you.

Snow is for . . .

making a snow angel or two.

Snow is for . . .

catching on the tip of your tongue.

Snow is for . . .

feeling like everyone is young.

Snow is for . . .

building just like you do with sand.

Snow is for . . .

creating a winter wonderland!

Learn MORE About SNOW

Snow is a form of ice that falls from clouds.

Ice is frozen water.

Snowflakes come in different shapes and sizes.

No two snowflakes are the same.

A heavy snowstorm is called a blizzard.